Cornerstones of Freedom

The Story of

THE JOHNSTOWN FLOOD

By R. Conrad Stein

Illustrated by David J. Catrow III

CHILDRENS PRESS ™

CHICAGO

Library of Congress Cataloging in Publication Data

Stein, R. Conrad.
  The story of the Johnstown flood.

  (Cornerstones of freedom)
  Summary: Describes the devastating tidal wave
that hit the city of Johnstown and several Pennsylvania
villages on Memorial Day, 1889, when the South Fork
Dam above the city collapsed as a result of spring
rains.
    1. Johnstown (Pa.) — Flood, 1889 — Juvenile litera-
ture.   Johnstown (Pa.) — Flood, 1889.   2.   Floods
I. Catrow, David J., ill.   II.   Title.   III.   Series.
F159.J7S75   1984   974.8'77   84-7824
ISBN 0-516-04680-2   AACR2

The people of Johnstown, Pennsylvania held a spirited celebration on Memorial Day, 1889. At the downtown square, a band blared patriotic music. A parade that included dozens of Civil War veterans marched up Main Street toward the cemetery. According to the town's Methodist minister, "The city was in its gayest mood, with flags, banners, and flowers everywhere."

But later that afternoon, a relentless rainfall drenched Johnstown. No one could remember a wetter spring than that of 1889. It was only the last week of May, but already that year rain or snow had fallen on more than one hundred days. In the countryside, farmers' fields had turned to ponds, and rural roads ran like rivers. The ground simply could not hold another drop of water. The people of Johnstown wondered if they would have to cope with another spring flood as they had many times before in the town's ninety-year history.

Johnstown, Pennsylvania, lies in a long narrow valley. It was settled in 1793 by a Swiss immigrant named Joseph Johns. For years it was a quiet farming village, until coal and iron deposits were discovered nearby. In 1861 an engineer named William Kelly introduced a new process of steel making in Johnstown. Soon large steel mills with tall smokestacks towered over the town. During the Civil War, the mills produced cannons. After the war, they churned out miles and miles of railroad tracks. By the 1880s, Johnstown rivaled Pittsburgh as Pennsylvania's leading steel producer.

People flocked to Johnstown for jobs in the steel mills. In 1889 the city and its neighboring suburbs held a population of some thirty thousand. Certainly Johnstown was not a pretty place. Few steel towns are. But the people there worked and played hard. A New York reporter once wrote that Johnstown "lived every moment. It swarmed with saloons. The place was accounted a good theater town by the profession."

Spring flooding plagued the city from its beginnings. Johnstown was built around a Y formed by two rivers—the Stoneycreek and the Little Conemaugh. In late summer the rivers were sluggish

and so shallow that a good jumper could skip over
them on rocks and never get his feet wet. However,
in spring they became tumbling, boiling torrents of
white water.

Spring flooding was so common in Johnstown that
the people almost expected it. The first recorded
flood struck the town in 1808. In the so-called
pumpkin flood of 1820, the Stoneycreek overflowed
its banks, picked up thousands of pumpkins from
farmers' fields, and deposited them on the streets of
Johnstown. Severe floods ravaged Johnstown on the
average of once every five years.

The people of Johnstown were victims of geography. First, their town was built along the banks of two rivers with a history of rampaging. Second, Johnstown sat at the mouth of a narrow valley so steep that it looked as if the bottom had simply dropped out of the earth.

While the people had learned to accept the flooding, they lived in fear of another more menacing body of water. In the mountains some fourteen miles east of town stood the South Fork Dam. It held a man-made lake that was three miles long, a mile wide, and sixty feet deep in some places. Incredibly, the dam was built on a mountaintop four hundred feet *above* the city of Johnstown. If that dam ever broke, the lake water would descend on Johnstown like a cleaver falling on the neck of a condemned man.

As Memorial Day ended, people lay awake listening to rain beat a steady tattoo on their roofs. By morning, both rivers had overflowed their banks, and the corner of Main and Market streets was under five feet of water. As the rain continued, rowboats replaced wagons as a means of transportation. All over town, families rolled up carpets and lugged valuable furniture up to attics.

High in the mountains outside of town a twenty-three-year-old engineer named John Parke paced the banks of the South Fork Dam. The forty-year-old dam had been built to provide water for a canal system that once ran most of the length of Pennsylvania. Railroads had made the canal obsolete and ownership of the dam passed to a wealthy country club. John Parke was director of a crew of workmen digging a sewer system to serve the luxurious summer homes along the lake's shores. But on the morning of May 31, 1889, Parke inspected the massive dam wall and trembled at what he saw. The wall was so wide that a two-lane wagon road ran along its top. However, the water of the lake now threatened to spill over the rim. And water oozed out of cracks along the dam's base.

Fearing disaster, Parke mounted a horse and rode two miles through the rain to the nearest village. There he told the telegraph operator to warn Johnstown and neighboring communities that the South Fork Dam was about to give way. Parke then galloped away so quickly that he failed to hear the telegraph operator shout to him that the wire to Johnstown was broken. She had no contact with the city.

Back at the South Fork, Parke saw water gushing over the top of the dam in steady, glassy sheets. The end came at 3:10 P.M. "The dam did not burst," Parke said later. "It simply moved away. The water gradually ate into [the wall] until there was nothing left but a frail bulwark. . . .This finally split asunder and sent the waters howling down the mountains."

Like a giant wave, the three-mile-long lake tumbled downhill into the narrow valley. Witnesses claimed that it took less than thirty minutes for the lake to empty. Rolling out of the highlands, this huge mass of water thundered toward Johnstown and the string of villages that lay before it.

The nearest village was a cluster of about thirty white frame houses called Mineral Point. The scene there defied the senses. At one moment the houses stood as unmovable as the earth itself. Then the mountain of water rolled over them. The entire village vanished. The roaring floodwaters simply erased it from the earth.

Below Mineral Point, a passenger train bound for Philadelphia was halted where rainwater had flooded the tracks. Among the passengers was a newlywed couple, Charles and Edith Richwood. Suddenly a man pointed out the train window and shouted, "My God! What is that?" Mr. Richwood later wrote, "Not more than a half-mile distant...we beheld a seething, turbulent wall of water, whose crests seemed mountain-high, filling the entire valley and carrying everything before it as cornstalks before a gale." Water filled the passenger car. In seconds the force of the current swept the entire train off the tracks and carried it down the valley. Richwood managed to break the train window. He and his bride found themselves "making the most dizzy and fantastic evolutions in our struggle to the surface. Up and up we went." Finally the Richwoods reached the surface, where they clung to the wreckage of a railroad car and miraculously survived the flood.

At its fastest pace, the battering ram of water pushed down the valley at forty miles an hour. But the water slowed as it was forced to veer left or right along the valley's twists and turns. Also, the rolling water picked up tons of debris—trees, boulders, telegraph poles, farmhouses, railroad cars—that acted as a brake on the flood's progress. At several narrow points in the valley, the wreckage clogged together to create temporary dams. However, each of these momentary dams burst and the combined mass of water and rubbish continued to rumble toward Johnstown.

At the village of East Conemaugh, a locomotive engineer named John Hess became a hero. He saw the tidal wave coming and raced his train into town, blasting an alarm on its whistle. Townspeople heard and immediately took to the hills. The floodwaters struck and ravaged the town and its railroad yards. Dozens of boxcars and an eighty-ton locomotive were swept up as if by the hand of a passing giant. Despite the devastation, few lives were lost in East Conemaugh, thanks largely to the quick thinking of John Hess.

The people of Woodvale were not so lucky. Without warning, the 120-foot-high mound of water and rubbish smothered the suburb. By this time, so much debris had gathered on the forward wall that many witnesses failed to see even a drop of water. Instead the mass looked like a moving mountain of junk. Houses in Woodvale were dashed to bits. Their wreckage added to the moving mountain, making it even larger. One of every three people in Woodvale was killed. The survivors clung to shells of houses and were taken on a wild ride toward Johnstown.

It was a hectic afternoon in Johnstown. Most people were busy bailing their city out of what was thought to be another nuisance of a spring flood. By four o'clock the skies actually had cleared and the water on the downtown streets was going down. People thought the worst was over. Then the torrent struck. George C. Gibbs, the editor of the *Johnstown Tribune*, saw the flood approaching. He later wrote, "The first appearance was like that of a great fire, the dust it raised. It came like a thief, and was upon us before we were aware....Johnstown was tumbling all over itself, houses at one end nodded to

houses at the other." Another eyewitness stood on a hilltop and watched the giant swell bury Johnstown. He told a reporter from the *New York Sun,* "In an instant the streets became black with people running for their lives. An instant later the flood came and licked them up with one eager and ferocious lap. The whole city was one surging and whirling mass of water, which swept away house after house with a rapidity that even the eye could not follow."

Sixteen-year-old Victor Heiser was in his family's half-flooded barn trying to tend to the horses when he heard a deep, earth-shattering roar. He splashed

outside and peered about, but could see nothing.
Meanwhile, the roar grew like the sound of an
approaching train. Victor raced up a ladder and
stood on the barn roof. To the west he saw what
looked like a monster wave washing in above the
rooftops. But how could it be a wave? Victor saw no
water—only a solid wall swarming with chunks of
houses, telegraph poles, and battered railroad cars.

Young Victor stood frozen to the barn roof, cer-
tain that in a moment he would be crushed like an
insect. But then he felt the barn under his feet being
wrenched from its foundation and pushed downhill.

Like a barrel in a pond, the barn began spinning end over end. Racing against the spin, Victor scrambled over the barn wall, then across a foundation beam, then up the next wall, and finally back onto the roof. To his left, a neighbor's house crashed into Victor's barn. He leaped for it and clung to its rooftop. When that house began to collapse, he jumped to another rooftop, and another, and another.

Finally Victor found a stable raft of wreckage. For fifteen minutes he had danced like a spider over a sea of junk. Now, for the first time, he saw water. And he saw other things that haunted him for the rest of his life. His friends and neighbors, also clinging to ruins, flashed by like faces in a nightmare. An Italian family that lived up the street came spinning along on what looked to be their kitchen floor. The man, his wife, and their two daughters evidently had been packing suitcases when a huge piece of wreckage toppled upon them, killing all four. On a rooftop racing through the current, Victor saw a black man who lived in his neighborhood. The man was on his knees, praying. The flood had torn off all his clothing. Somehow his deep bass voice boomed even louder than the flood. Victor bowed his head and silently joined his neighbor in prayer.

Another Johnstown resident caught in the whirlpool was eight-year-old Gertrude Quinn. With her aunt, an infant cousin, and a nurse, Gertrude sought refuge in the Quinns' attic three stories above the street. Years later, Gertrude wrote what she saw while peering through the attic window: "Screams, cries and people running; their white faces looking like death masks. . . .Bells were ringing, the whistles in the mills were sounding a last warning."

The floodwaters pounced on the Quinns' frame house, splitting it open at the seams. "This is the end of the world," Gertrude's aunt said. "We will all die together." The aunt began to pray, but Gertrude hoped to save herself. A tomboy, she could shinny up trees even faster than some boys. A great crack yawned open in the attic wall. Gathering all her courage, Gertrude dived out. She could not have prayed for a greater miracle than what happened next. She landed on a piece of wreckage containing someone's empty bed. The mattress was soaked with mud, but was surprisingly soft. Riding on top of this bed, she was swept along with the rest of the rubble that was once the city of Johnstown, Pennsylvania.

At the far end of Johnstown stood a giant struc-

ture which the townspeople called simply Stone Bridge. It had seven sixty-foot-high spans and accommodated four railroad tracks side-by-side. Had it been in the direct path of the floodwaters, it no doubt would have been knocked down and carried off. But the towering bridge was situated in such a way that the flood first had to smash off the side of a mountain and then veer toward it.

Because the mountain absorbed most of the flood's force, an unusual event occurred at the bridge. Tons of debris piled up in front of the seven spans. This tangle created a leaky but unpassable dam. So the rampaging floodwaters came to a halt at the city limits of Johnstown. However, the bizarre dam meant even greater woes for the people. In effect, the dam created a new lake. Now the city was buried under twenty to thirty feet of standing water on which floated tons of rubble.

Hundreds of dazed survivors drifted upon this new lake. One of them, close to Stone Bridge, was sixteen-year-old Victor Heiser. To his amazement, he discovered he could climb over the jagged wreckage and reach solid ground on the hills surrounding the city. Once on the ground, Victor headed for Stone Bridge, where he thought he saw smoke. All over the lake, other survivors crawled over the floating debris toward shore. Many were badly injured. But everyone able to move inched toward high ground.

In all parts of the devasted city, ordinary citizens performed heroic rescues that later became legendary. A man named Edward Deck heard the cries of a woman and a child trapped underneath a tin roof. He ripped at the roof until his hands were covered with blood, but he freed the victims. Miles away from Stone Bridge, a railroad laborer named J.W. Esch tied a rope around his waist and repeatedly dived into open swirling water. By the end of the evening, he had fished out sixteen people and hauled them to dry ground. Hundreds of other fantastic rescues were never written about and went unnoticed by history.

One of those rescued was eight-year-old Gertrude Quinn. Her raft of wreckage spun madly in open water far from Stone Bridge. She caught sight of corpses in the current, but turned her head to avoid looking at them. Night was falling and Gertrude was terrified. A white frame house with a man on top sailed by her. Gertrude yelled for help. The man hugged the chimney of the house and said nothing.

Gertrude shouted at him, "You terrible man! I'll never help you."

Next Gertrude passed a roof crowded with people. A steelworker named Maxwell McAchren saw her predicament, dived into the swirling water, and swam toward her raft. Twice the treacherous current sucked him under. Finally McAchren climbed onto the wreckage with Gertrude and both were carried downstream. Close to a hill, Gertrude saw a black man and a white man leaning from the window of a hillside house. With long poles they reached for the people washing by. One of the men shouted to Gertrude's companion, "Throw that baby over here!" Gertrude was flung through the air and landed in the arms of George Skinner, whom she later described as "a gallant colored fellow."

From her refuge in the hillside house Gertrude spent the evening gazing down at the swirling sea of debris. Years later she described the scene: "At the window I beheld what once was our town....I saw nothing but water, and two or three big fires reflecting over the waves looking for all the world like ships burning at sea."

Fires often accompany such disasters as earthquakes and hurricanes. But rarely does a fire follow a flood. That dreadful night, however, the people of Johnstown suffered through the twin tragedies of flood and flame. The mass of floating debris pressing against Stone Bridge somehow caught fire. Investigators later theorized that it was set by coal stoves still burning in the mangled kitchens of houses.

The flames curled up Stone Bridge and swept over the floating wreckage. Injured people caught in the rubble screamed for help. Rescuers risked their lives trying to free people trapped under layers of ruins. Among those who battled to save lives was young Victor Heiser: "I joined the rescue squads and we struggled for hours trying to release [the people] from this funeral pyre, but our efforts were tragically hampered by the lack of axes and other tools. We could not save them all. It was horrible to watch helplessly while people, many of whom I actually knew, were being devoured in the holocaust."

An eerie night descended on Johnstown. Hellish sounds pierced the darkness. The flames at Stone Bridge crackled. Screams from the fire's victims echoed over the moans of injured people everywhere. And bone-chilling sounds came from hundreds of homeless dogs prowling the hillsides overlooking the new lake. The dogs, unable to under-

stand the sudden shattering of their world, wandered without direction, howling dismally.

The unearthly night finally ended. In the morning, searches began for missing children, parents, and friends. Strangers approached each other and asked such questions as, "Have you seen my five-year-old little towhead? He stands about so high." The morning brought some joyous reunions. "What strange meetings they were," wrote one survivor. "People who had hardly known each other before the flood embraced one another, while those who had found relations rushed into each other's arms and cried for the very gladness that they were alive. All ordinary rules of decorum and differences of religion, politics, and position were forgotten."

The morning light also enabled the people to grasp the enormity of their loss. Nearly every house in the city was wrecked. The ruins were buried under water, mud, and junk. Corpses lay everywhere. There was scant food, no clean water, and no medical supplies. Smoke poured from Stone Bridge, but at least the fire there was dwindling.

Rather than cry over their fate, the men and women of Johnstown went to work. A meeting was called at Alma Hall, one of the few city buildings to survive the floodwaters. A minister named Beal claimed that he reached the hall by "walking and jumping from one house or roof or boxcar to another, sometimes compelled to bridge over deep water spaces with loose boards or planks." At the meeting a new government was formed, work teams were organized, and the weary people began the enormous job of digging out.

Help came from outside communities. Early that first morning, neighboring farmers hitched up wagons and brought milk cans full of fresh water and baskets of food to Johnstown. As word of the disaster spread, it triggered an outpouring of charity from other American cities. Schoolchildren contributed nickels and dimes to buy relief supplies

for Johnstown. In just one week, $600,000 was collected in New York City alone. Boston sent $14,000 and Kansas City $12,000. American millionaires, including John Jacob Astor and Jay Gould, wrote large checks to the relief fund. Money even came from the Lord Mayor of Dublin, Ireland, and the Sultan of Turkey.

To the city came a volunteer crew of doctors and nurses led by a tireless sixty-seven-year-old woman named Clara Barton. She had served as a nurse during the Civil War and in 1881 had founded the American Red Cross. The Johnstown Flood marked the first time the Red Cross served victims of a disaster. Under Miss Barton's supervision, the Red Cross set up a field hospital and tended to hundreds of injured and homeless persons.

Arriving with the relief workers were scores of newspaper reporters. They came to Johnstown expecting to find widespread disorder and rioting. Instead, they discovered the people of the city behaving in a marvelously civilized manner. Disappointed, some of the reporters recklessly made up their own stories. FIENDS IN HUMAN FORM read a headline in the *New York Herald*. The accompanying story told of ghoulish "foreigners" who scavenged among the dead, cutting off fingers in order to steal gold rings. Other reporters claimed that mobs of angry townspeople were lynching "foreign grave robbers." But some newsmen told the truth. Alfred Reed of the *New York World* cabled his newspaper, "No lynchings. I warned you last night not to print wild rumors."

Only after many months did the people of Johnstown attempt to count their losses. The toll was staggering. Because many hundreds of bodies never were found, the actual number of people killed by the flood is unknown. The official death toll was set at 2,209. Some fifteen hundred homes were destroyed, and $17 million in property was lost or damaged.

Despite these losses, the people rebuilt their city in an amazingly short period of time. But Johnstown remained a victim of its geography. The city suffered through more tragic floods. In 1936 a flood took twenty-five lives and caused $40 million in property damage. After that disaster, the federal government spent millions of dollars widening the banks of Johnstown's two rivers. The project, completed in 1943, was supposed to put an end to the awful flooding. But in 1977, the Conemaugh River overflowed; the resulting flood killed eighty-five people in the Johnstown area.

Within a century, three major floods ravaged Johnstown. Still, somehow, the people's spirit remained positive. After the 1977 flood, a city official looked over the damage and said, "We dug ourselves out in 1936 and in 1889. We'll do it again."

And they did.

About the Author

R. Conrad Stein was born and grew up in Chicago, He enlisted in the Marine Corps at the age of eighteen, and served for three years. He then attended the University of Illinois, where he received a bachelor's degree in history. He later studied in Mexico and earned a master of fine arts degree from the University of Guanajuato. Mr. Stein is married to Deborah Kent, who is also an author of books for young readers. They have a baby daughter, Janna.

The study of history is Mr. Stein's hobby. Since he finds it to be an exciting subject, he tries to bring the excitement of history to his readers. He is the author of many other books, articles, and short stories written for young people. Mr. Stein wishes to thank the staff of the Johnstown Flood Museum for their cooperation in his research for this book.

About the Artist

David J. Catrow III was born in Virginia and grew up in Hudson, Ohio. He spent three years in the United States Navy as a hospital corpsman and subsequently attended Kent State University, where he majored in biology. He is a self-taught illustrator. Mr. Catrow currently lives in Springfield, Ohio with his wife Deborah Ann and daughter Hillary Elizabeth. He is an editorial cartoonist for the *Springfield News-Sun*. The artist would like to thank Deborah for her constant support and inspiration.